AI and the Legal Field
Automation, Ethics, and Intellectual Property

Table of Contents

Chapter 1. Introduction

As artificial intelligence becomes increasingly refined, it is altering the landscape of nearly every industry. One of these is the legal profession, where the impact of AI promises to be both deep and far-reaching. In our special report on "AI and the Legal Field: Automation, Ethics, and Intellectual Property," we delve into these complex nuances in an easy-to-understand way. Without getting lost in intricate technical jargon, we unpack how automation is revolutionising legal processes; question the ethical boundaries of using AI in law; and explore the emerging challenges surrounding artificial intelligence and intellectual property. Designed to provide a comprehensive view for both professionals in the industry and curious individuals alike, this report assures to shed light on the future of law in the era of AI - an integral read for anyone wanting to stay ahead of the exciting transformations that lie ahead.

Chapter 2. The Rise of AI in the Legal Profession

The advent of artificial intelligence (AI) is undeniably transforming the legal sector and redefining traditional frameworks. While the industry initially faced resistance to technological integration due to its reliance on human intuition and discretion, this hesitation is gradually retreating in the face of AI's compelling and increasingly robust capabilities. As the role of AI intensifies, it is creating profound modifications in the structure, services, operations, and ethics of the legal profession.

2.1. The Confluence of Law and Technology

The legal profession is complex and demands a high level of knowledge, reasoning, interpretation, and judgement. The advent of AI has the potential to expedite mundane and repetitive tasks, freeing up time for legal professionals to focus on more complex and intricate matters. AI's capability to learn and scale, combined with its precision and speed, is yielding unprecedented outcomes, making it an incredibly powerful tool for the legal field.

Machine learning, an application of AI, stands at the forefront of reshaping legal practices. Through large-scale pattern recognition, machine learning can identify legal strategies, predict litigation outcomes, and even draft contract outlines. The application of predictive algorithms simplifies and enhances the discovery process, aiding legal teams in scanning and filtering large volumes of data for relevant information.

Natural Language Processing (NLP), another arm of AI, is also unlocking new avenues in law. By processing and analysing human language in a meaningful way, NLP allows for automated document review, legal research, and contract analysis, marking a significant departure from conventional methodologies.

2.2. Automation – Reshaping Legal Practices

AI-driven automation is creating more efficient workflows and decreasing human labour in time-consuming tasks. For instance, document review and due diligence activities take up the majority of a lawyer's time. However, with automated tools powered by AI and machine learning, these tasks can be executed with greater accuracy and in a fraction of the usual time.

AI is also transforming legal research. Lawyers often spend countless hours poring over case laws, reading and researching legal proceedings to build or defend a case. Today, AI-powered research tools can comb through hundreds of thousands of legal documents in seconds, identifying pertinent case laws, marking significant precedents, and delivering comprehensive research reports.

Additionally, AI aids in risk management and compliance, two crucial aspects of corporate law. AI can maintain real-time tracking of legislation changes, ensuring businesses comply with up-to-date regulations, thereby reducing the risk of hefty fines and penalties.

2.3. Opportunity and Job Displacement

A prevalent concern regarding AI in law is job displacement. However, while AI will automate many routine tasks, there is growing consensus that it is unlikely to replace lawyers. Instead, AI can be seen as a potent tool that complements and enhances the capabilities of legal professionals.

Adopting AI will open new career opportunities related to designing, developing, implementing and maintaining these systems. Therefore, AI may change traditional legal roles, not eliminate them.

2.4. Ethical Implications: A New Frontier

While AI undoubtedly has advantages, it also opens new ethical frontiers. Its use in determining punishments, predicting recidivism rates, and making other critical legal decisions, raises serious concerns. Importantly, the decision-making processes of AI algorithms can be opaque and difficult to explain, leaving room for biases that can affect judgment and fairness.

This hybrid system of human and AI professionals will undoubtedly necessitate a revised ethical framework to guide interactions and manage risks.

2.5. Navigating Intellectual Property Laws

AI's expansion into creative fields presents new challenges for intellectual property (IP) laws. As AI evolves to create original content, it raises questions about ownership, copyright, and IP laws' applicability. For example, if an AI creates a piece of music or writes a novel, who owns the rights to that work? Conversely, since AI relies on large datasets for learning, there are pressing questions about violating IP rights when those datasets include copyrighted or proprietary material.

2.6. The Legal Sector: Poised For Revolution

With the rise of AI, the legal system is on the brink of permanent change. This revolution may have legal professionals resisting wholesale adoption, yet with the vast potential advantages, it is clear AI is set to become an integral component in the industry.

While the journey is ongoing, converging AI with law promises a future where repetitive tasks are automated, case outcomes are predicted with higher precision, and ethical and IP conundrums are navigated with greater care. Ultimately, AI in the legal profession is not just about technology integration; it is a transformative journey towards a more efficient, precise and just legal system.

Chapter 3. Understanding Automation in Legal Processes

In recent years, we have witnessed an explosion of technological advancement that's revolutionizing how industries operate. One particular area of interest that has experienced this transformation is the legal profession, where automation is carving out a significant and multifaceted role.

3.1. Role of Automation in Legal Processes

Automation in the legal field, simply put, is all about using technology to carry out tasks typically performed by humans. The primary aim is to streamline processes, reduce human error, bolster productivity, and enhance overall efficiency. Tasks like document review, contract management, legal research, due diligence, and prediction of legal outcomes – traditionally handled manually – are being transformed by automation in unprecedented ways.

The legal sphere is laden with repetitive, rule-based tasks that, when performed manually, can consume an immense amount of time and resources. Storing, sorting, and retrieving countless documents, drafting routine legal paperwork, and other such tasks can be daunting and labor-intensive. Automation acts as a solution to many of these challenges, enabling law firms to handle these tasks more efficiently.

3.2. Automation in Legal Research and Document Review

Legal research and document review are two areas where automation is demonstrating its power. Traditionally, these tasks have been labor-intensive and costly, but automation can significantly cut down on the time and resources required.

Legal research, for instance, often saw attorneys sifting through countless case laws, legal journals, statutes, and other materials in search of relevant information. Now, AI-powered tools can automate this process using Natural Language Processing (NLP) to sift through extensive databases, providing comprehensive, relevant, and timely research findings in a matter of seconds.

Likewise, document review – the process of uncovering relevant evidence in legal documents – can be substantially automated. Software that uses Machine Learning algorithms can review and categorize documents based on relevance and context, thereby making this process efficient and less error-prone. Automation not only reduces the time consumed but also minimizes the risk of oversights that can potentially have serious legal implications.

3.3. Automation in Contract Management and Due Diligence

In areas such as contract management and due diligence, automation has also made a significant impact. Contract management involves creating, examining, and monitoring a contract's lifecycle. Traditionally, law firms might have used spreadsheets for this task - a method prone to errors and inefficiencies. However, contract management software can automate many aspects of this process, providing capabilities such as generating consistent legal language, tracking obligations and timelines, and predicting risk outcomes.

Due diligence – an integral part of transactions like mergers and acquisitions – involves a thorough investigation to evaluate the business aspects, legal implications, and potential risks involved. This is typically a painstaking and labor-intensive task. Automated due diligence solutions employ advanced AI algorithms to review thousands of pages of documents, sift through data, and provide crucial insights faster and with greater accuracy than manually possible.

3.4. Predictive Analytic Tools

Finally, one other notable impact of automation in law is the advent of predictive analytics tools. These tools leverage AI and machine learning to analyze past case data and predict potential outcomes of ongoing cases. By identifying patterns and making correlations, these tools can offer invaluable insights into case strategies, providing lawyers with a competitive edge.

3.5. Advantages and Challenges of Automation in Law

While the advantages of automation in law are numerous, they do not come without challenges. Among the benefits, we can cite increased efficiency, productivity, and accuracy, ancillary to cost and time savings. These can enable law firms to offer better service to clients and focus their human resources on more strategic and higher-value tasks.

The challenges, though, are also considerable. One major concern revolves around the loss of jobs, as automation could replace human roles in certain tasks. The transition from traditional methods to modern automated processes may also pose teething issues. Plus, there are significant security and privacy matters since much sensitive legal information is digitized and thus can be vulnerable to cyber threats.

In conclusion, while automation is no magic bullet, it's reshaping legal processes in groundbreaking ways. It's essentially a powerful tool that, if employed judiciously, could both catapult the legal profession into the future and significantly augment the value delivered to clients. Like all technological advancements, automation in law involves a balance of benefits and risks. To truly leverage its potential, legal professionals must stay informed and proactive, mastering these tools while also adapting to their evolving implications.

Chapter 4. Ethical Considerations in AI-Led Law Practices

The explosion of AI technologies in the past decade has raised a plethora of ethical considerations, changing the legal landscape forever. Many legal practices are embracing digital advancements to streamline their services and increase efficiency. However, the use of AI is not without its ethical implications, requiring careful thought and consideration.

4.1. The Automation Versus Human Judgement Dilemma

In the realm of AI-led law practices, one conspicuous ethical dilemma is the tension between automation and human judgement. Effective legal work usually requires a mix of data analysis, critical thinking, and a deep understanding of human behaviour — areas where AI can potentially excel but also places where it might falter. AI lacks human characteristics such as empathy and conscience which typically guide moral judgements in conventional law practice.

AI can analyze vast amounts of legal data quicker and arguably more accurately than a human. But it's important to remember that these systems are designed, built, and controlled by humans, who are inherently fallible. Bias can inadvertently be coded into algorithms due to assumptions or stereotypes held by the developers. This can result in skewed decision-making when applied to legal cases.

Thus, while automation of legal processes can enhance efficiency, there remains the question about the role of human judgement in interpreting and applying the law correctly. Incorporating fail-safe measures to ensure unbiased AI operation, regular 'health checks' for algorithms, and legal practitioners acting as a final filter can contribute towards mitigating risks and holding the genuine control power.

4.2. AI and The Implications for Privacy

Concerns around privacy rank high on the list of ethical considerations around AI-led legal practice. Machine learning algorithms can be used to glean insights from massive datasets including, but not limited to, historical case data, personal background information, or social media activity. However, the intense scrutiny of numerous data points raises privacy concerns.

A classic conundrum is how much personal data AI should be allowed to mine and analyze, and whether data anonymization truly provides sufficient protection in an era marked by rapid technological advancement. Handling this data requires extremely robust protection measures to prevent breaches, which could result in severe harm to clients if their potentially sensitive information is exposed.

Balancing data collection with privacy protection will continue to be a key issue as AI-infused legal practices develop, potentially necessitating stricter regulation and standards governing the use of AI in law.

4.3. AI and Accountability in Law

Perhaps one of the most controversial ethical concerns surrounding AI in law relates to accountability. The question arises as to who should be held responsible if a machine learning model makes an incorrect, unfair, or unethical decision.

A key challenge is that many AI systems operate as 'black boxes,' where decision making processes are complex and often not transparent, even to those who created them. This can make it difficult to determine how a particular decision was reached, complicating the issue of accountability.

Moreover, when decisions made by AI lead to unfavorable outcomes or legal errors, it's unclear whether the fault lies in the machine learning model, the data it was trained on, or the operators who implemented the system. Hence, establishing a clear accountability framework is not only an ethical necessity, but fundamental to maintaining public faith in AI applications within legal practices.

4.4. The Future: Cultivating Ethical AI in Law

As AI becomes increasingly ingrained in the legal sector, cultivating a culture where legal tech developments are guided by robust ethical considerations becomes paramount. Strategies could include increasing transparency around AI decision-making, establishing clear accountability frameworks, and ensuring the responsible handling of data.

Furthermore, legal professionals might necessitate training in AI ethics to allow them to navigate this complex landscape and make informed decisions about how they employ AI in their work.

One thing is clear – AI holds significant potential for the legal profession. However, harnessing its power must not come at the expense of ethical conduct. Recognizing and addressing these considerations will help shape a legal future where AI contributes positively and ethically to justice and equity.

Chapter 5. Navigating AI and Intellectual Property Challenges

Artificial intelligence has rapidly planted its roots in almost all aspects of life. As it continues to evolve, new challenges emerge within the realm of intellectual property (IP). Notably, the existing IP frameworks are put to test as they were not designed with autonomous AI in mind.

5.1. AI's Role in Creating Intellectual Property

Artificial intelligence has transcended the line of aiding humans to independently creating intellectual property. In a study, conducted by researchers from the University of Surrey, two AI systems named DABUS received patent rights for an advanced food container and a special device for search and rescue missions. This significant advancement is quickly becoming a global phenomenon, posing new challenges for traditional patent laws. These laws did not foresee a future with machines creating or ideating items of human-level innovation and creativity.

Looking more closely, DABUS is a unique AI created to simulate human ideation by interconnecting numerous artificial neural networks. Remarkably, DABUS has managed to produce designs for applicable, novel inventions - something that opens a Pandora box of IP issues. After all, who is the inventor here: the human mastermind behind the AI or the AI itself?

5.2. Patent Rights and AI

Patent law as we know it operates on the fundamental principle that the inventor holds the patent rights. However, the advent of AI creating intellectual property draws upon this principle, raising some pressing questions. If an AI develops a patentable invention, can it be constituted as an inventor? And if so, who would have the rights over the patent?

According to most national and international patent laws, an "inventor" is typically an individual - a human being. These laws never envisaged machines or AI-led software as inventors, leaving us in an unprecedented situation. As such, getting past this hurdle requires a reinterpretation of the patent statute or, more radically, an overall reform at the legislative level.

In the DABUS case, the US Patent and Trademark Office (USPTO) and the European Patent Office (EPO) declined the notion of an AI inventor, reinforcing that under current patent law, 'a machine cannot be an inventor'. This forms a crucial existing viewpoint in navigating the maze of AI and IP.

5.3. Copyright and AI's Creative Outputs

While the patent discourse dominates the AI intellectual property landscape, we shouldn't neglect AI in the realm of copyright. It's not just technical and scientific innovations that AI can produce – it can also generate creative works like music, art, and literature.

We must confront the same question here: who owns the rights to these AI-generated creations? Is it the AI programmer, the AI user, the AI itself, or does nobody hold the copyright as it was generate by a non-human?

Existing copyright laws in several jurisdictions foreshadow tangible difficulties for AI-generated creations. The UK Copyright, Designs, and Patents Act 1988, for instance, suggests that in the case of a computer-generated work, the author is the individual 'by whom the arrangements necessary for the creation of the work are undertaken'. This possibly could assign copyright ownership to the programmer or user of the AI, but it remains open to interpretation and needs more defined regulations.

5.4. Initiating Effective Regulations for AI and IP

Existing IP frameworks are insufficient to aptly handle the extraordinary issues emanating from the pervasive use of AI. What is needed is a new legal framework that acknowledges autonomous machines' creative abilities, adequately protecting human stakeholders' rights while promoting innovation.

At an individual level, nations must strive to develop domestic regulations to mediate these novel challenges. Japan, for instance, has already started this process, having proposed guidelines in 2019 regarding inventions made by AI and IoT technologies.

On a larger scale, international cooperation is required for harmonization of regulations across jurisdictions. Just as international treaties like the Berne Convention standardize copyright laws globally, a similar global agreement might be necessary for AI and IP, ultimately enabling worldwide, uniform adjudication of AI-driven IP disputes.

5.5. Conclusion: The Way Forward

Navigating AI and IP challenges is a complex task, with growing urgency given the rapid evolution of AI technologies. Our future teems with the unavoidable influence of AI, and we must accordingly reshape our legal frameworks and mindset. A revamped approach to IP; further engagement with philosophers, AI scientists, and legal professionals; and global cooperation are all important steps towards a comprehensive understanding of AI and its impact on intellectual properties.

While we look forward to these changes, it is crucial for legal luminaries, innovators, and policy-makers to nurture a dynamic conversation surrounding AI and IP to keep up with the fast-paced AI evolution. By doing so, we will ensure that the legal field is adaptive, covering the gaps left by previous technologies, and ensuring equitable distribution of rights and innovation promotion.

Indeed, the intersection of AI and intellectual property isn't just a legal challenge, but a layered socio-technical issue. Understanding and addressing this requires an intricate look at the broader implications of AI on society and the economy. By embracing these complexities, we can foster an environment conducive to striking a balance between protecting rights and nurturing innovation.

Chapter 6. The Impact of AI on Legal Counsel and Advice

Artificial intelligence has been disrupting various sectors for some time now, and the legal profession is no exception. Law firms and departments worldwide are continually adapting to these novel technologies, refining their practices and launching new initiatives. This chapter offers a detailed exploration of the ways in which AI is impacting legal counsel and advice.

6.1. AI in Legal Research

One of the first areas where AI has made inroads is legal research. Traditionally, this has been a high-volume task that requires significant time and expenditure. The need to sift through mountains of legal documents, case records, articles, and statutes made research a daunting challenge. However, artificial intelligence, through machine learning and Natural Language Processing (NLP), has revolutionized this process.

AI-powered platforms can analyze a large volume of data at a much quicker pace and with impressive accuracy. They can scan documents, recognize patterns, extract relevant information, and even predict potential outcomes. Platforms like Westlaw Edge and Casetext employ AI to help lawyers navigate complex legal databases. This allows legal practitioners to access the information they need in less time, leading to increased efficiency.

While AI aids in dramatically reducing the time lawyers spend on research, it also enhances the quality of the outcomes. AI's ability to discern connections or patterns that might be easily missed by humans is beneficial in building a strong argument for a case. Therefore, legal professionals can take advantage of AI tools to carry out comprehensive, accurate, and efficient research.

6.2. AI and Contract Review

Contract review is another domain that significantly benefits from AI. In traditional practice, reviewing stacks of documents is not just time-consuming but also prone to human errors. AI, with its capability to analyze huge data sets accurately and quickly, has been a game-changer.

Tools such as Kira Systems, Legal Robot, and LawGeex use AI to review and analyze contracts. These platforms can extract vital data points, identify errors or anomalies, and highlight potential risks. They can even help draft contracts by using previous documents as templates, thereby saving lawyers from the monotony of repetitious work.

These enhancements not only offer convenience but also impact a firm's bottom line. Implementing AI for contract reviews reduces the margin of error, streamlines the workflow, and thereby results in substantial cost savings.

6.3. AI and Litigation Prediction

One of the significant breakthroughs of AI in the legal field is predictive analytics. Specific software, such as Lex Machina, uses machine learning algorithms to predict the outcome of legal disputes. These platforms analyze past cases, extraction patterns, and use them to predict potential litigation outcomes.

While it's a relatively new tool, AI in litigation prediction has potential both in terms of time and cost efficiency. It can analyze enormous amounts of data in a fraction of the time a legal team would need and is not subject to fatigue or errors that humans might be. So while AI tools aren't infallible predictors of court outcomes, they provide valuable insights to legal counsels, thereby helping formulate effective strategies.

6.4. AI and Legal Ethics

With all its remarkable contributions towards enhancing legal practice, there's a conversation brewing about AI and legal ethics. The application of artificial intelligence brings forth several ethical considerations. For instance, can a lawyer rely completely on AI for research without risking professional negligence? How does one ascertain data handled by AI tools is stored and processed ethically and securely?

Addressing these concerns requires a thorough understanding of AI and comprehensive regulatory guidelines. All AI applications must emphasize transparency, explainability, and fairness. It's equally crucial for legal professionals using these tools to fully comprehend how they work to mitigate possible risks.

6.5. Intellectual Property and AI

Finally, there's a growing debate surrounding AI and intellectual property law. As AI systems become more sophisticated, they're creating artworks, inventing new products and writing pieces independently. This raises a fundamental question - who owns the rights to AI-generated work?

At present, IP laws are built around human innovation. Therefore, addressing these dilemmas requires rethinking our existing legal frameworks to accommodate AI's unique abilities and challenges it poses.

In conclusion, the impact of AI on legal counsel and advice is ever-increasing. While AI presents challenges and ethical questions that need grappling with, its benefits in terms of efficiency, accuracy, and cost-saving are undeniable. As legal professionals all over the world adapt to this novel technology, the face of legal practice as we know it is set to change drastically.

Chapter 7. Integrating AI in Courthouses: Prospects and Pitfalls

Artificial intelligence (AI) promises to bring transformative change to courthouses and the legal ecosystem, from streamlining processes to predicting outcomes. However, this innovative technology also comes with a set of novel challenges, requiring judicious assessment and implementation.

7.1. Benefits & Potential of AI in Courthouses

AI technology, with its capacity to analyze vast amounts of information swiftly and accurately, presents significant opportunities for operational efficiency and improved justice delivery in courthouses. Increased automation could automate the straightforward and repetitive tasks currently performed by legal professionals, thus freeing them for more consequential roles.

The ability of AI to assist in e-discovery is another significant advantage; it can sift through voluminous data, highlighting relevant information while discarding the immaterial. This is not only quicker and potentially more accurate than human-performed e-discovery but also remarkably cost-effective. The cost of litigation often escalates due to heavy discovery burdens, and AI could significantly trim these expenses.

AI can further benefit courts by predicting potential outcomes based on past rulings. Deep learning algorithms can analyze hundreds or even thousands of previous cases to identify patterns, allowing lawyers to build an informed strategy. This prospective analysis provides a more precise view of potential litigation outcomes and could guide litigation and settlement decisions.

Additionally, AI applications could digitize and automate many courthouse administrative processes. AI-powered bots could schedule hearings, manage case flow, and even facilitate remote proceedings, bringing unprecedented fluidity to court operations. Empowering judicial administrations with AI could lead to more expeditious and transparent proceedings and facilitate universal access to justice.

7.2. Pitfalls & Challenges of Implementing AI in Courthouses

Despite the clear advantages, the implementation of AI in courthouses is not without substantial challenges. It's essential to consider potential pitfalls critically, understanding and addressing them in the design and application of these technologies.

Firstly, the risks of AI-driven decision-making on fairness and due process are paramount. AI systems analyze patterns based on past data. This practice can perpetuate and amplify biases present in the historically captured data, potentially leading to unjust outcomes. Additionally, these systems are considered "black boxes," meaning their decision-making process is often impenetrable, which runs counter to the legal principle of transparency.

Secondly, there is a risk of erroneous results. No AI system is infallible, and any mistakes can have serious repercussions on the lives of individuals and the consistency of the justice system. Responsibility for AI-driven mistakes in judgement or identifiable instances of bias is difficult to assign, particularly when the technology's operation is not entirely understood by its human overseers.

Thirdly, the issues of privacy and data security should not be overlooked. Given the sensitive nature of legal data and the severe implications of its unauthorized access or misuse, stringent measures must be in place to protect it. AI technology also necessitates processing vast amounts of data to make accurate predictions, which magnifies these data privacy concerns.

7.3. Future Directives

AI holds great promise for improving court processes, but careful consideration must be taken to keep its application under ethical and legal parameters. A shift towards transforming the culture in courthouses to be more tech-friendly is requisite, with intensive training programs being an integral part of this process. Further, a collaborative development approach involving all stakeholders, including legislators, judges, lawyers, and technologists, is essential for the successful and ethical integration of AI into the legal system.

As we unlock the potential of AI for courthouses, its implementation should be guided by a cornerstone principle of law – it ought to be rooted in comprehensible rules and be just and equitable. As such, maintaining balance between the innovative disruption and preserving justice's fundamental principles will be integral to the effective deployment of AI in our courthouses.

As AI continues to evolve, the legal sector must adapt to leverage its capabilities fully. Being vigilant to the changes brought about by AI will ensure that the legal profession continues to protect fundamental rights and uphold justice in the face of technological advancements.

Chapter 8. Legal Transcription and Documentation in the Age of AI

For years, legal professionals have spent countless hours transcribing audio records of court proceedings, depositions, and client meetings. This exhaustive and meticulous task, while undeniably crucial, has been ripe for innovation. The advent of Artificial Intelligence now opens up a world of possibilities in the domain of legal transcription and documentation. Today, let's delve into how this technological shift is changing the game.

8.1. Transcription and Documentation: An Overview

Legal transcription is about turning spoken language into written form and is considered vital in legal matters. Legal documents, however, are much more than just transcribed conversations. They represent decisions, actions, and evidence, forming the backbone of the justice system. These documents are drafted with precision. The use of AI can significantly streamline these tasks, enhancing efficiency, accuracy, and productivity.

8.2. AI and Legal Transcription

With AI in the mix, what used to take hours can now be accomplished in minutes. Automatic speech recognition (ASR) technology, a core component of AI, can transcribe faster and, to a certain extent, more accurately than human transcribers. This technology is designed to understand and convert spoken language into text. Providing legal professionals with quick access to search, edit, and share transcripts can speed up the legal process.

AI-driven transcription software also enables users to customize their transcriptions. The software has built-in capacity to learn legal terminology, making it better over time. However, like every AI technology, ASR is not without limitations. Accents, environmental noise, overlapping speech, and unfamiliar words can challenge its accuracy. Therefore, while ASR substantially reduces the burden of transcription, a human eye is still required to guarantee the accuracy of the end product.

8.3. AI and Legal Documentation

Beyond transcription, AI is also making strides in legal documentation - streamlining document review, legal research, and contract analysis. By employing Natural Language Processing (NLP), AI can easily scan and interpret vast volumes of legal documents.

AI can undertake legal research rapidly, accessing online databases and swiftly identifying relevant statutes, case laws, or secondary sources. It can also analyze legal documents by assessing the risk factors or provisions in a contract. Once again, while AI can power through volumes of documentation far more quickly than human professionals, the lawyer's discerning eye will still be needed to identify nuanced context and make ultimate decisions.

8.4. Ethical Considerations

Despite the clear benefits, the use of AI in legal transcription and documentation also stirs ethical questions, primarily around privacy and confidentiality. Law firms handle incredibly sensitive information, and the use of AI tools potentially exposes this information to breaches and cyber attacks. Therefore, it's crucial for law firms using AI technology to prioritize robust cybersecurity measures.

Another underlying concern relates to the potential for AI transcription errors impacting the legal processes. Should an AI misrepresent or miss an important fact in transcription or documentation, it could have serious consequences for a case or a client. Reassuringly, the law dictates that professionals must still check, refine, and approve AI-crafted documents, placing a check on its influence.

8.5. Intellectual Property Concerns

As much as AI contributes to the legal profession, it also creates new challenges related to intellectual property (IP). Ever-present IP concerns involve the creation of new documents or new technologies. For instance, if an AI system creates a document, who owns the rights to that document? The IP rights around AI-generated work remain in a grey area, requiring further discussion and resolution.

8.6. The Road Ahead

AI is unquestionably changing the face of legal transcription and documentation. By reducing time-consuming tasks, it allows legal professionals to focus on tasks that necessitate a human touch, like strategizing and counseling. Yet, its seamless integration demands vigilance regarding ethical considerations and IP rights. As we move ahead, striking the right balance between technology and human involvement will be crucial to revolutionize the legal landscape further.

To conclude, the onset of AI in the domain of legal transcription and documentation is a significant leap towards automating routine tasks. However, the success of this revolution truly lies in creating symbiosis between AI and human expertise, where machines handle repetitive tasks, and humans focus on providing strategic legal insight.

Chapter 9. AI and Legal Research: Efficiency Unleashed

Legal research entails a comprehensive search for precedent, statutes and case law to provide relevant evidence for court pleadings, legal memoranda, or scholarly papers. Traditionally, lawyers had to sift through physical records to gather this information - a labour-intensive and time-consuming task.

AI is transforming this aspect of the legal profession considerably. Innovative technologies are reducing human error, enhancing accuracy, minimising mundane work, and delivering more efficient and effective results. Essentially, AI is unlocking significant efficiencies in legal research.

9.1. AI and Document Review

One domain seeing a significant impact from AI is document review. Lawyers frequently need to review vast amounts of data for e-discovery during litigation and investigations. Actions such as finding relevant information, evaluating the context, identifying patterns, or flagging privileged or sensitive content — all typically handled by a legal team — are rather daunting.

AI can automate the process using natural language processing (NLP) and machine learning. NLP enables algorithms to understand and interpret human language in a valuable way, while machine learning algorithms can learn and improve from experience. Combined, they allow AI systems to read and analyse documents, highlight essential information, and even predict a document's relevance based on past decisions made by lawyers.

Over time, the AI learns from the feedback of legal practitioners, improving itself, refining its methodologies, and becoming more effective with every case. This ultimately leads to cost savings, better time management, and increased accuracy in legal services.

9.2. Predictive Analytics in Law

While predicting judicial decisions is not an exact science, AI brings the power of predictive analytics to the legal world. It can analyze data from past cases, consider the case in question, evaluate the judge and legal proceedings histories, and predict a case outcome based on these factors.

For instance, Supreme Court Analytics is a tool developed to forecast decisions of the U.S Supreme Court. It analyses massive amounts of data about the court's justices and their voting patterns to make predictions. This information could be invaluable for creating legal strategies, managing client expectations, and making informed decisions on whether to pursue a case or settle out of court.

9.3. Legal Chatbots

AI technology has paved the way for legal chatbots. These sophisticated AI programs interact with users, answer their questions, and assist them with various legal matters. They are able to provide quick and cost-effective services, which is particularly useful for basic legal services that do not require human intervention.

For example, the chatbot "DoNotPay" helps users dispute parking tickets without the need for a lawyer. It asks questions about the situation, guides the user through the appeal process and drafts letters to send to the relevant authorities. This not only makes law more accessible to the public but also spares lawyers from monotonous tasks.

9.4. Legal Research Platforms

Legal research platforms enhanced with AI capabilities are making significant inroads in the industry. Platforms such as ROSS Intelligence, Casetext, and Westlaw leverage AI and cognitive computing technologies to improve legal research.

For example, ROSS Intelligence uses machine learning algorithms to understand and answer questions posed by legal professionals in natural language, review multiple legal documents quickly to deliver solutions, and continuously improve from feedback - enhancing the legal research process.

9.5. Faults and Shortcomings of AI

Even as AI technologies offer numerous advantages in legal research, it is not without shortcomings. AI relies heavily on the quality and quantity of data it has been trained on. Thus, an AI system will only be as good as the data it learns from. This can lead to problems if the AI is trained on biased data or lacks access to critical information.

Additionally, most AI technologies are interpretive; they are not capable of understanding or interpreting legal principles, which is a human skill mastered through years of legal training and experience. Therefore, while AI can assist in legal research, it cannot replace the nuanced judgement of experienced lawyers.

Finally, the ethical issues around AI in law are yet to be fully addressed. There's a need to ask if AI should be allowed to predict deicisons, ethical consequences of such predictions, and the responsible use of AI in law.

9.6. The Road Ahead

The fusion of AI and law, specifically in legal research, is a revolutionary advancement. While AI can already aid with document review, provide predictive analytics, support via legal chatbots, and enhance legal research platforms, it is bound to go further.

The technologies will continue to evolve, becoming more refined and efficient. AI could be developed to understand legal principles and reasoning, make legal predictions with more accuracy, and potentially transform the way law is understood and practiced.

However, with these advancements comes a set of challenges that will need to be addressed, particularly around ethical norms and principles. The legal profession and policymakers will need to play an active role in shaping the future of AI in legal research, ensuring that it is used responsibly and effectively. Legal professionals will also need to adapt and develop skills to interact with and make the best use of these new technologies.

Undoubtedly, AI has unleashed a new level of efficiency in legal research, forever changing the legal landscape. However, it will always exist to augment human intelligence, rather than replace it. It's a powerful tool, poised to support the legal profession rather than making it obsolete, enriching the field with more accuracy, speed, and cost-effectiveness.

Chapter 10. Adapting Legal Education for the AI Era

Future lawyers will not only need to understand the fundamentals of jurisprudence but also the basics of programming and data science. This can partly be achieved through presenting the intersection of law and AI across various subdomains in the legal profession. Through this integrative approach, they can gain a bifocal lens, seeing both the legal and technical perspectives, an essential aspect as we transition into the digital era.

10.1. Rethinking Course Curriculum

Law schools have a monumental task ahead of them. They need to sufficiently equip the next generation of lawyers with the skills to navigate an industry experiencing a digital revolution. To achieve this, we need to revamp our teaching methodologies and core curriculums, blending law with technology-focused education.

The new syllabus should encompass subjects such as coding, data analytics, AI, machine learning, blockchain, and cybersecurity. These subjects will introduce law students to the basic principles of digital automation, the rudiments of programming and key understanding of how AI functions within the legal sector.

Beyond merely updating course syllabi, law schools should consider adopting alternative teaching strategies that nurture problem-solving skills, critical thinking, and tech-savviness. Project-based learning, for instance, can be tremendously beneficial. Through interdisciplinary projects that demand the integration of law and technology, students will begin to understand the convergence of these two disciplines.

10.2. Incorporating Experiential Learning

Experiential learning will play a crucial role in merging the legal and tech world. Building partnerships between law schools and AI-related industries could pave the way to internships and hands-on training opportunities. In this real-world context, students would grapple firsthand with the challenges posed by the marriage of law and AI, as they assist with drafting AI-related legal documents, explore how AI can be used to automate legal processes and more.

10.3. Training in LegalTech Platforms

As part of the education process, law students should be introduced to the latest LegalTech software available in the market. Platforms that summarize court judgments, those conducting legal research, AI-driven contract analysis tools, or software automating routine legal tasks can provide students a sense of the practical side of how AI is transforming the legal industry.

10.4. Ethics and the AI Legal Landscape

Law schools should offer a focused exposure on ethics under the influence of AI technology. As AI becomes more integral to the legal profession, there is an increasing need for lawyers who can adeptly navigate the ethical and legal landscape surrounding it. Students must understand the potential risks AI technology can generate, including issues of data privacy, confidentiality, and the unbiased application of law.

10.5. Preparation for the Unpredictable

It is essential to teach students to equip themselves for roles that may not yet exist. As the tech/AI revolution advances, new roles will likely be created in the legal field, and education should prepare students to adapt. Fostering a culture of continued learning and development, and emphasizing adaptability and resilience, will serve to ensure that the future generation of legal professionals can handle the dynamic nature of the legal landscape.

10.6. Economic Reality and Law School Selection

Students should be given an honest view of the current job market and future career prospects. Aspiring law students must be educated about the increasing role of AI and technology in the legal sector before choosing a law school or their specialized areas of practice. Such transparency will equip students with the knowledge they need to make informed decisions regarding their future.

Adapting law education to facilitate the growth of AI is a challenging but necessary process. By building an integrative learning environment, law schools can prepare our future legal professionals to navigate the constantly evolving intersection of law and technology, marking the advent of a truly transformative era for the legal sector.

Chapter 11. The Future Outlook: AI's Role in Law by 2030

With each passing year, artificial intelligence (AI) is becoming more deeply embedded in various industries. From transforming the manufacturing process to reshaping service delivery, the promise of artificial intelligence is immense and far-reaching. One such industry is the legal profession. As we look towards 2030, we are confronted with the belief that AI will have a profound influence on the law. This chapter explores several aspects of that future outlook in depth.

11.1. Automation of Legal Processes

Already, we are witnessing a shift in the way routine legal work is accomplished. AI research and development have made it possible for legal documents like contracts, legal briefs, and other paperwork to be drafted, reviewed, and edited in an automated fashion. By 2030, we can expect these processes to be significantly more sophisticated, with AI being able to handle tasks that have the highest level of complexity, possibly even outpacing human ability to process such tasks.

The automation of these processes will drastically reduce the time spent on tedious paperwork, improve accuracy, and cut costs in legal proceedings. More importantly, this will allow lawyers to focus on more critical aspects of their job, such as legal strategizing, client counseling, and court arguing. The role of the lawyer in this context will change, making the profession more strategic and advisory as opposed to administrative.

11.2. The Ethical Boundaries of AI in Law

As we march towards a world where AI possesses a more significant role in the legal profession, we face ethical questions regarding privacy, accountability, and job displacement.

Privacy issues are paramount when considering the adoption of AI in law. By 2030, AI will be capable of processing massive amounts of personal information to aid in litigation processes and offer predictive legal advice. Balancing this capability with individuals' right to privacy will undoubtedly become a major ethical challenge.

Moreover, the question of accountability in the event of AI mistakes will pose significant challenges. With AI carrying out sophisticated legal tasks, there will inevitably be a potential for mistakes. Deciding who is responsible for these mistakes—man or machine—will remain a key inquiry for jurists and policy-makers.

AI's impact on jobs will also demand ethical considerations. The fear that AI will displace jobs is valid to an extent. While AI will surely take over some tasks, it will also create new job opportunities, especially in AI development, implementation, and oversight.

11.3. AI and Intellectual Property

As AI becomes more sophisticated, questions surrounding intellectual property (IP) rights increase. There are already instances where AI has created works that stretch the traditional boundaries of IP laws, such as music, art, and even scientific research papers.

The challenge lies in determining who owns the rights to these creations. Current IP laws attribute ownership to the human creator. What happens when an AI system creates something without direct human intervention? Who owns the rights to AI-created works?

These questions will need definitive answers based on updated IP laws by 2030.

11.4. The Intersection of AI and Legal Regulations

Regulating AI in the legal realm is another pressing issue that will cause much debate by 2030. Governments worldwide will have to enact regulations to guide AI usage in law to ensure ethical and fair practices. Regulatory efforts will need to focus on preserving human oversight, ensuring transparency and accountability, and setting boundaries for the degree of autonomous decision making permitted to AI legal systems.

11.5. Conclusion: AI and the Future of Law

As we look to the future, it is clear that AI is going to play a substantial role in the legal landscape by 2030. It promises a more efficient, cost-effective, and sophisticated legal industry, but brings with it a host of ethical and legislative challenges.

The key to maneuvering through these challenges will be in finding a balance between embracing AI's transformative potential and preserving the core principles of our legal systems. This will entail active participation from various stakeholders, including legal practitioners, AI specialists, and policy makers, who will need to work together to redefine laws and the legal profession in this age of artificial intelligence.

www.ingramcontent.com/pod-product-compliance
Lightning Source LLC
Chambersburg PA
CBHW072221290526
45794CB00007B/2833